SKILLED TRADE CAREERS
CARPENTERS

by Gary Sprott

Rourke
Educational Media

A Division of
Carson
Dellosa
Education

BEFORE AND DURING READING ACTIVITIES

Before Reading: *Building Background Knowledge and Vocabulary*

Building background knowledge can help children process new information and build upon what they already know. Before reading a book, it is important to tap into what children already know about the topic. This will help them develop their vocabulary and increase their reading comprehension.

Questions and Activities to Build Background Knowledge:

1. Look at the front cover of the book and read the title. What do you think this book will be about?
2. What do you already know about this topic?
3. Take a book walk and skim the pages. Look at the table of contents, photographs, captions, and bold words. Did these text features give you any information or predictions about what you will read in this book?

Vocabulary: *Vocabulary Is Key to Reading Comprehension*

Use the following directions to prompt a conversation about each word.

- Read the vocabulary words.
- What comes to mind when you see each word?
- What do you think each word means?

Vocabulary Words:
- apprentice
- blueprint
- contractor
- lumber
- sustainable
- whittle

During Reading: *Reading for Meaning and Understanding*

To achieve deep comprehension of a book, children are encouraged to use close reading strategies. During reading, it is important to have children stop and make connections. These connections result in deeper analysis and understanding of a book.

Close Reading a Text

During reading, have children stop and talk about the following:

- Any confusing parts
- Any unknown words
- Text to text, text to self, text to world connections
- The main idea in each chapter or heading

Encourage children to use context clues to determine the meaning of any unknown words. These strategies will help children learn to analyze the text more thoroughly as they read.

When you are finished reading this book, turn to the next-to-last page for **After Reading Questions** and an **Activity**.

TABLE OF CONTENTS

ON THE JOB

Do you enjoy building models? Are you the type of person who likes to know how things are built? Would you like to use cool tools—and your imagination—to transform something simple into something beautiful?

Awesome! Let's explore what it takes to make the grade as a carpenter!

A Forest of Jobs!

There are more than one million carpenters in the United States. That number is rising as more homes are built for a growing population. Wow, we're going to need a lot of nails!

Carpenters build and repair structures made of wood or other materials. They build walls and cabinets and install doors and windows. Carpenters may follow an architect's **blueprint** to plan their work. They measure and cut wood for floors, staircases, and other building features.

blueprint (BLOO-print):
a model or detailed plan of something being built

Carpenters work with a **contractor** to build new houses and office buildings. They fix older buildings by installing new and improved features, such as flooring.

Some carpenters build temporary wooden structures that help other workers do their jobs on large construction projects, such as skyscrapers and bridges. They are called rough carpenters.

contractor (KAHN-trak-tur): a person who agrees to do a particular job, especially in the building industry

Do you enjoy puzzles? Carpenters are always thinking two steps ahead when installing floors.

Ancient Egyptians used tools for working with wood. They carved wooden coffins for their mummies!

Trees have been around longer than humans. So, it's no surprise that people have been using wood to build homes, boats, and furniture for thousands of years. Ancient civilizations developed simple tools to cut, carve, and chisel.

"Wood" You Believe It?

Ever knock on wood for luck? Some say the superstition began long ago. People knocked on tree trunks to call the good spirits they believed lived in the forest!

Trees and forests give us life. They produce oxygen, remove harmful carbon from the atmosphere, and give shelter to wildlife.

Carpenters can help protect the planet. They can use materials from **sustainable** sources, such as bamboo. And using recycled wood means cutting down fewer trees!

sustainable (suh-STAY-nuh-buhl): easily replaced; capable of being used for a long time without being wiped out or without harming the environment

Forests cover about one-third of the land in the U.S.

WHAT'S IN MY TOOLBOX?

Hard-hitting hammers. Fast-firing nail guns. Drills and sanders. Band saws, circular saws, and jigsaws! A carpenter's toolbox is a wonder of useful equipment. But, regardless of the job, there's one little thing no carpenter can do without—a pencil usually kept behind the ear!

Carpenters spend all day handling razor-sharp saw blades and chisels. They carry heavy tools and supplies. Safety is their top priority at all times! A carpenter needs a hardhat, goggles, and tough but flexible gloves. Another must-have: steel toe boots to protect their toes from falling objects.

Careful Up There!

Carpenters often work high above the ground. They must balance, like a cat, on beams and roofs. Carpenters wear body harnesses secured to a line that stops them from dropping to the ground if they fall.

Carpenters use different types of **lumber** for different jobs. Floors have to stand up to stomping feet, spilled juice, and toy car crashes! So, a hardwood like oak might be best. For outdoor projects, a softwood like cedar can fight off rot from weather and termites.

lumber (LUHM-bur): wood that has been sawed into planks or boards for use in building things

Carpenters visit lumber yards to have wood measured, cut, and delivered.

LEARNING THE TRADE

If you think education is important for carpenters, well, you've hit the nail on the head!

A high school diploma is needed for this trade career. Classes such as mathematics, geometry, and mechanical drawing are useful.

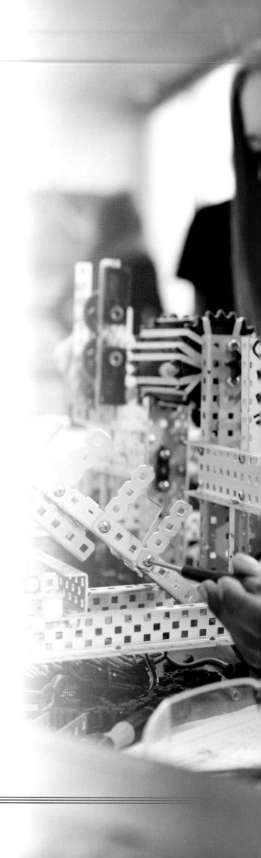

A fascination with carpentry can begin as a hobby. Perhaps you enjoyed using a wooden airplane kit you got for your birthday. Maybe a relative or neighbor showed you how to **whittle** wood, or to make a birdhouse. A mighty career can grow from a little seed of interest!

whittle (WIT-uhl): to make or carve something by cutting or shaving small pieces from wood with a knife

Carving Up the Competition!

A block of wood, a pocket knife, a timer, and a dash of creativity! Those are the ingredients for a whittling contest. Woodcarvers compete around the world, winning prizes for their wooden works of art.

Extra time on your hands?
You could be whittling it away
with a woodcarving hobby.

Technical colleges, or trade schools, offer carpentry programs. Students learn how to handle tools safely and practice installing doors, windows, and cabinets. They study building codes and use computers to design projects. They also learn how to use first aid in an emergency.

High school woodworking classes are great for learning the basics of being a carpenter.

Apprentices learn about carpentry under the expert eye of skilled professionals.

Carpenters begin their career as an **apprentice**. They spend several years learning on the job and in the classroom. Experienced carpenters train them, starting with simple tasks. After completing an apprenticeship, a carpenter may be known as a journeyman or journey worker.

apprentice (uh-PREN-tis): someone who learns a skill by working with an expert

Carpenters must continue to sharpen their skills—just like their saws! Unions and other workers' groups offer training in specialized areas. The United Brotherhood of Carpenters and Joiners of America has a 1.2 million-square-foot (111,500-square-meter) training center in Las Vegas, Nevada.

Brothers and Sisters!

Groups such as Sisters in the Brotherhood (SIB) encourage women to become carpenters. SIB provides education, leadership training, and support to aspiring and experienced women carpenters.

Education and training are the building blocks to a rewarding career as a carpenter.

MEMORY GAME

Look at the pictures. What do you remember reading on the pages where each image appeared?

INDEX

AFTER READING QUESTIONS

1. How many carpenters are there in the U.S.?
2. Why did people long ago knock on tree trunks?
3. How can carpenters help protect the planet?
4. What is special about a carpenter's work boots?
5. What is the United Brotherhood of Carpenters and Joiners?

ACTIVITY

Does your family own a toolbox? Ask a parent or adult relative to show you how some of the tools work. Staying safe at all times, see what it feels like to drive a nail home or fasten a screw. Afterward, take a closer look at the furniture in your house. Which of the tools would you need to build that furniture?

ABOUT THE AUTHOR

Gary Sprott is a writer in Tampa, Florida. He has written books about ancient cultures, plants, animals, and automobiles. In high school, Gary made a wooden rack for coffee mugs. It was pretty good—in a Charlie Brown Christmas tree kind of way.

www.rourkeeducationalmedia.com

PHOTO CREDITS: page 1: ©xresch / Pixabay; page 1: ©3alexd / iStock; page 3: ©ronstik / iStock; page 4: ©EHStock / iStock; page 5: ©XiXinXing / iStock; page 6: ©jhorrocks / iStock; page 9: ©Suz Waldron / shutterstock.com; page 10: ©The Yorck Projec / Wikimedia; page 11: ©Givaga / iStock; page 13: ©Pgiam / iStock; page 14: ©artisteer / iStock; page 15: ©andresr / iStock; page 16: ©SasaStock / shutterstock.com; page 19: ©NoSystem images / iStock; page 21: ©monkeybusinessimages / iStock; page 23: ©photoschmidt / iStock; page 25: ©SDI Productions / iStock; page 26: ©monkeybusinessimages / iStock; page 28: ©AndreyPopov / iStock; page 29: ©PIKSEL / iStock

Edited by: Madison Capitano
Cover design by: Rhea Magaro-Wallace
Interior design by: Book Buddy Media

Library of Congress PCN Data

Carpenters / Gary Sprott
(Skilled Trade Careers)
   ISBN 978-1-73163-831-1 (hard cover)
   ISBN 978-1-73163-908-0 (soft cover)
   ISBN 978-1-73163-985-1 (e-Book)
   ISBN 978-1-73164-062-8 (e-Pub)
Library of Congress Control Number: 2020930242

Rourke Educational Media
Printed in the United States of America
01-1942011937